Amazing Creatures

Lynn Huggins-Cooper

QEB Publishing

Published in the United States by
QEB Publishing, Inc.
23062 La Cadena Drive
Laguna Hills, CA 92653

www.qeb-publishing.com

Library of Congress Control Number: 2008011764

ISBN 978 1 59566 563 8

Author: Lynn Huggins-Cooper
Edited, designed, and picture researched by:
  Starry Dog Books Ltd.
Consultant: Sally Morgan

Publisher: Steve Evans
Creative Director: Zeta Davies
Senior Editor: Amanda Askew

Printed and bound in China

Picture credits
Key: t = top, b = bottom, l = left, r = right, c = center,
FC = front cover, BC = back cover.

A = Alamy, C = Corbis, D = Dreamstime.com, F = Fotolibra,
G = Getty Images, ISP = iStockphoto.com, P = Photolibrary,
PS = Photoshot, S = Shutterstock.com, SDB = Starry Dog Books,
SPL = Science Photo Library.

1 S/ © Patsy A. Jacks; 2–3 D/ © Markross; 4t D/ ©
Twwphoto, 4b P/ © Daniel Cox; 5 D/ © Alisongoff; 6t
G/ © Tim Laman, 6b F/ © David Knowles; 7 G/ © Roine
Magnusson; 8t © Dr Rafe M. Brown, 8b P/ © Wells Bert &
Babs; 9 C/ © Gary Bell/zefa; 10 D/ © Jolka100; 11t S/ © Dino,
11b C/ © Saed Hindash/Star Ledger; 12t SPL/ © Rod Planck,
12b C/ © Nigel J. Dennis/Gallo Images; 13 C/ © Gavriel
Jecan; 14t C/ © Hans Reinhard/zefa, 14b SPL/ © Nicholas
Smythe; 15 P/ © David M. Dennis; 16t C/ © Joe McDonald,
16b C/ © Markus Botzek/zefa; 17 S/ © Patsy A. Jacks; 18t
S/ © Michael Lynch, 18b ISP/ © Holger Mette; 19 P/ © M
Delpho; 20t S/ © clearviewstock, 20 b P/ © Stan Osolinski; 21
S/ © Vova Pomortzeff; 22t C/ © Wolfgang_Thieme/dpa, 22b
ISP/ © James Richey; 23 ISP/ © Elzbieta Sekowska; 24t ISP/ ©
Anna Yu, 24–25 C/ © Nigel J. Dennis; Gallo Images; 25t G
/ © Timothy G. Laman; 26 P/ © Michael DeYoung; 27 C/ ©
Frans Lanting; 28 D/ © Destonian, 28–29 SDB/ Nick Leggett.

Contents

Really wild!

The animal world is full of amazing creatures. Some look cute, but the sweetest-looking animals may be very fierce. Creatures that look scary may be gentle and shy. Other animals are very colorful and extraordinary-looking, which helps them to survive in their natural environment.

▲ *Weasels are fierce predators. They have beautiful fur like a cat, but you cannot stroke them!*

Bad behavior?

Animals kill other animals because they need to eat. Sometimes, animals attack people, and we think of this behavior as vicious. All wild animals can be dangerous. If a man enters a bear's territory, the bear may follow its instincts and attack, just as it would if any other wild animal threatened its territory. Its behavior is not vicious, it is natural wild animal behavior.

◀ *Bears will attack if they are surprised, feel threatened, or are protecting their territory or* **cubs**.

▶ Leafy sea dragons are a type of fish. They are related to sea horses. Their leafy **appendages** may look strange, but they help sea dragons to hide among floating seaweed.

Smelly animals

Some animals really stink! However, the smells do have a purpose. A stinky smell can make an animal more attractive to its mate, or it may keep predators at a safe distance.

▲ *Moonrats have a long, sensitive nose for detecting smells. They hiss at other moonrats on their territory.*

Moonrats

Moonrats live in the rain forests and **mangrove swamps** of Sumatra, Borneo, and the Malay Peninsula. They mark their **den** with a liquid that smells like rotting onions or garlic. The smell warns other moonrats and predators to stay away from their territory.

Polecats

Polecats live in woodland areas of Europe, Asia, and North Africa. They mark their territories with a foul-smelling liquid, made in **glands** at the base of the tail. People once used the word "polecat" to describe someone with a character as foul as the polecat's smell.

◀ *Polecats mostly hunt at night. Their keen sense of smell helps them to detect rabbits, rats, birds, snakes, frogs, and fish.*

Foul fact!

In the early 1900s, musk oxen were hunted nearly to extinction *for their meat and hide*. Now, however, they are protected by law.

Musk ox

The musk ox lives in cold regions, in Greenland and northern Canada. Males, called bulls, produce a strong-smelling liquid in glands just under their eyes. To release the smell, the bull rubs its face on trees and bushes. The smell attracts females, who can detect it from a long way off.

▶ *The musk ox has long hair with a thick layer of wool underneath.*

Animal Stickers

Some animals are sticky and others can stick to things using **suction**. Long, sticky tongues allow some animals to catch their food. Others use suction pads to move around or cling onto branches or rocks.

▲ *When alarmed by a predator, the black-spotted sticky frog puffs itself up and turns its back to the predator, showing off two large spots. To the predator, this view looks like a snake's head.*

Black-spotted sticky frog

The black-spotted sticky frog lives in the rain forests of South East Asia. At night, it hunts for insects on the forest floor. The frog releases a sticky slime when it is threatened, making it an unpleasant meal for predators.

Numbat

The numbat, or banded anteater, lives in the forests of south-west Australia. It uses its nose to track down **termite mounds**. When it finds one, the numbat pokes its long, sticky tongue into holes in the mound. The termites stick to the tongue and the numbat has a feast!

◄ *The numbat eats about 20,000 termites every day.*

Crown-of-thorns starfish

The crown-of-thorns starfish lives in warm seas and feeds on coral. Thousands of tiny tube feet underneath its arms help the starfish to move around. The feet have suction cups that allow the starfish to cling onto rocks.

▼ *The crown-of-thorns starfish is covered in long, poisonous spines.*

Foul fact!

The crown-of-thorns starfish is usually about the size of a dinner plate, but can be as big as a car tire.

Disease carriers

Many animals carry diseases that can be passed on to each other, such as **mange** in dogs. Some animals carry diseases that, rather scarily, can be passed on to humans, too.

Dogs and cats

Dogs and cats carry **parasites**, such as **tapeworms** and **roundworms**, which live inside them. The eggs of the parasites pass out in the **feces** of the dog or cat. People can end up with these parasites, too, if they get the eggs on their hands by touching dogs, and then eat without washing their hands. Regularly "**worming**," or treating, your dog or cat kills the worms.

◀ *It is important to wash your hands after playing with your dog or cat so that you don't pick up any diseases.*

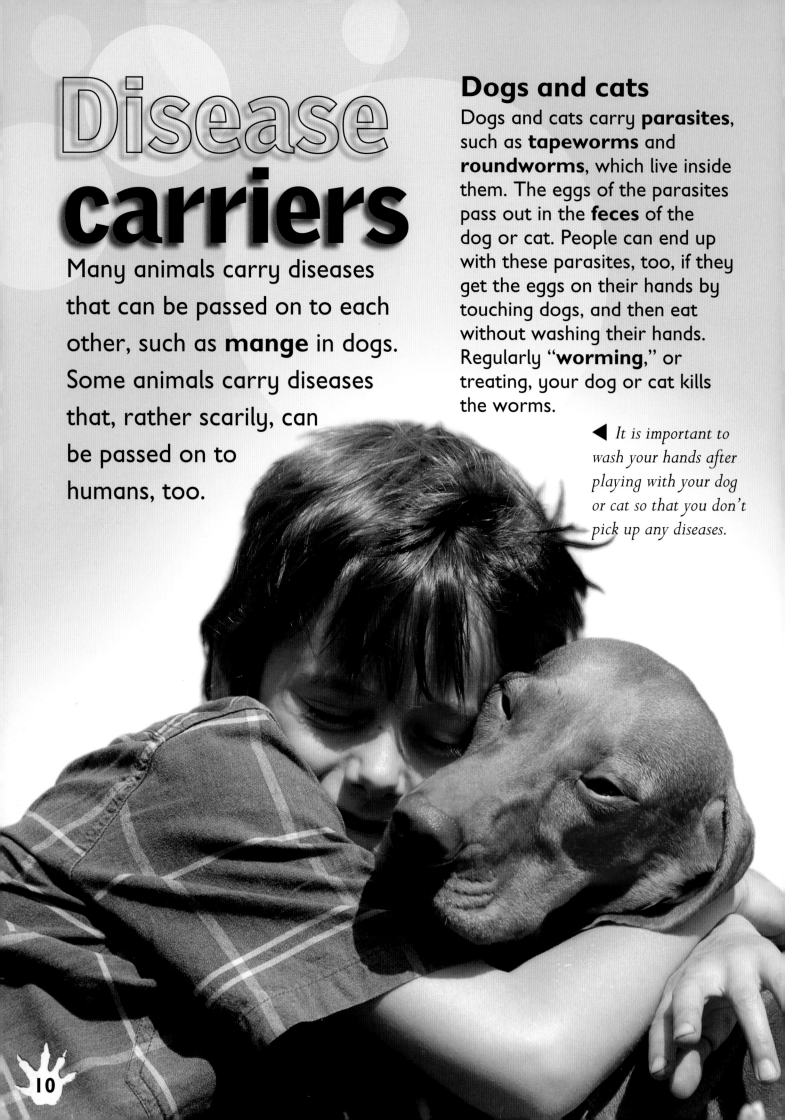

Foul fact!

In the 16th century, pigeon feces was used to make gunpowder, and was considered to be very valuable!

Pigeons

Many towns around the world have large numbers of pigeons. The birds can carry a disease that affects their lungs and the lungs of people. Symptoms of the disease are mild in pigeons, but can be serious in humans. People catch the disease by breathing in dust containing specks of the birds' feces. **Bacteria** in the feces can give a person a fever.

▲ *Be careful not to hold pigeons if you feed them, as this carries a health risk and is not a good idea.*

Rats

Rats live almost everywhere that people live. They spread many diseases, including food poisoning, **typhus**, and **bubonic plague**. In the 14th century, the plague became known as the Black Death. It was passed on to humans by infected fleas from the rats. The Black Death may have killed as many as 50 million people in Europe.

▶ *Rats eat the food in our trash. Many live near us, in the **sewers** beneath the streets.*

Nasty noses

Some animals have amazing noses, which they use to seek out food. They may smell their **prey** from a long way off, or use their sensitive noses to detect movements made by their prey.

▲ *The star-nosed mole's tentacles help it to identify prey by touch, as it is blind*

Star-nosed mole

The star-nosed mole of North America looks like an ordinary mole—except for its nose. 22 fleshy tentacles stick out from the nose and wriggle constantly. They help the mole to feel movements in the ground made by its prey, such as worms.

Aardvark

The aardvark lives in Africa in the area south of the Sahara Desert. It has a long **snout**, which it uses to sniff out its food—ants and termites—as it walks along at night. It may walk as far as 18.5 miles in one night, pressing its nose to the ground to pick up their scent. It also listens for any sound of movement made by the termites.

▶ *When an aardvark digs a burrow or breaks into a termite mound, it can squeeze its nostrils shut to keep out the dust.*

▶ *The nose of the male proboscis monkey can be up to 5.5 inches long. It makes the monkey's warning calls louder.*

A male proboscis monkey pushes its nose out of the way when it eats!

Proboscis monkey

The proboscis monkey is named after the large, wobbly nose, or "proboscis," of the male monkey. It is thought that the large nose helps the male to attract a mate. It lives in the swampy mangrove forests of Borneo, and wades through the water on its back legs. This makes it very unusual, as most monkeys move around using all four legs.

Poisonous animals

There are many types of poisonous creature around the world. Some animals use **venom** for defense. Others use it to catch larger prey.

▲ *The duck-billed platypus has a flat bill like a duck's beak, a furry body, and strong limbs that help it to swim and dig.*

Duck-billed platypus

The duck-billed platypus lives in eastern Australia. It eats frogs, fish, and insects. The male platypus has a **spur** on each of its back legs, which holds a strong poison. If threatened, the platypus stabs its attacker with a spur and injects the poison. The poison is strong enough to kill a dog.

Solenodons

The two species of solenodon are both **endangered**. They live on the Caribbean islands of Hispaniola and Cuba. When a solenodon attacks its prey, such as a spider, poisonous **saliva** flows into its victim along grooves in its lower front teeth. The poison stuns the prey, making it easier to grasp.

◀ *Solenodons run on their toes, and often trip over if they try to run too fast.*

▼ *Here, a diamondback rattlesnake is having its venom removed. The venom is used to make antivenom, a medicine used to treat snake bites.*

Pit vipers

The diamondback rattlesnake is a type of pit viper that is common in North and Central America. Pit vipers are venomous snakes. They can sense body heat, which enables them to sneak up on their prey at night. They bite to kill, but will also bite in self-defense. Their hollow fangs inject poison into their prey.

Foul fact!

Many pit vipers are hunted and killed for their skins, which are used to make shoes and belts.

Vicious animals

Animals, such as killer whales, tigers, and bears, are well known for being fierce. However, the world is also full of small, vicious creatures that hunt their prey aggressively.

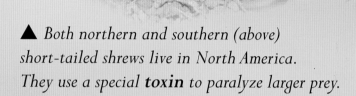

▲ *Both northern and southern (above) short-tailed shrews live in North America. They use a special **toxin** to paralyze larger prey.*

Northern short-tailed shrew

The northern short-tailed shrew is small, but very fierce! It needs to eat three times its body weight each day, so it spends its time hunting for insects, spiders, worms, and snails.

▶ *Weasels prey on mice, voles, frogs, birds, and rabbits. They eat eggs, too!*

Weasels

Weasels live mainly in the **northern hemisphere**. The weasel is a savage hunter. Its long, slender body allows it to follow its prey into small burrows. When excited, weasels do a strange, hopping war dance. Some **biologists** believe they perform the dance to confuse their prey.

Foul fact!

Various words are used to describe a group of weasels including a gang, pack, confusion, and boogle!

Tasmanian devil

The Tasmanian devil looks like a small bear and is very vicious. It uses its powerful jaws to crack bones and tear fur and flesh, before eating the lot. As well as feeding on carrion—animals that are already dead—it also eats the **larvae** of some types of beetle, and attacks poultry.

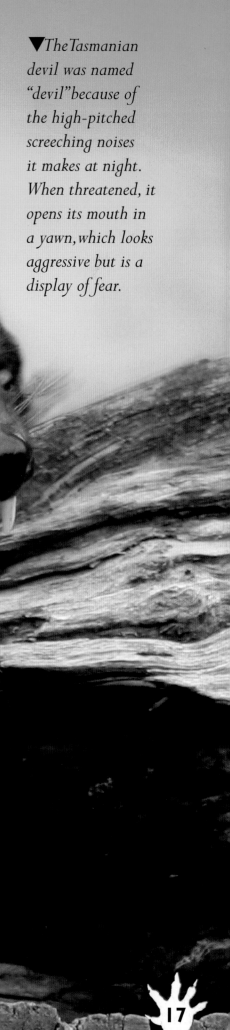

▼The Tasmanian devil was named "devil" because of the high-pitched screeching noises it makes at night. When threatened, it opens its mouth in a yawn, which looks aggressive but is a display of fear.

Sneaky animals

Some animals use sneaky methods to catch their prey or to escape from predators. They may use disguises, move quietly, or use clever tricks.

▲ *The vampire bat quietly creeps along the ground up to its prey, such as a cow or a pig.*

Vampire bats

Vampire bats are found in Africa and South America. The common vampire bat is able to walk, jump, and hop. This means it can creep up to its prey and hop onto its body. As it bites, the bat's saliva enters the wound and makes the animal's skin go numb. The animal does not know it has been bitten.

Tarsiers

Tarsiers are related to monkeys and lemurs. They are found on islands in South East Asia. Tarsiers have good eyesight and hunt mostly at night, jumping onto their prey, which includes insects, birds, and snakes. They pounce and grab the animal with their paws.

◀ *Tarsiers have large pads at the end of long fingers, to help grip branches and prey tightly.*

Many people think of raccoons as pests because the animals spill the garbage from cans in streets and gardens.

Raccoons

Raccoons are very sneaky. Their specially adapted paws can open latches and doors. Their black eye patches make them look like masked bandits—and they can act like them, too! They often steal food from houses, cars, and campsites.

▲ *Raccoons often rifle through trash cans in search of food.*

Terrifying tongues

Some animals have an amazing tongue. It may be forked, sticky, or just incredibly long. Tongues can be used for digging insects from the ground or grabbing leaves and branches.

▲ *An echidna hunts by poking its nose into the ground, leaving behind cone-shaped nose prints.*

Echidnas

Echidnas, or spiny anteaters, live in Australia, Tasmania, and New Guinea. They have small nostrils and a tiny mouth at the end of their long, tubelike beaks. They eat ants and termites, which they catch with their long, sticky tongue.

Okapi

The okapi is brown with a stripy **rump** and legs. It is related to the giraffe. A shy animal, it lives in the dense forests of the African Congo and was only discovered in 1901. The okapi uses its long, black tongue to grab leaves and branches and pull them into its mouth.

◄ *The okapi's tongue is is 14 inches long. It is as sensitive and flexible as a human hand.*

Sun bear

The sun bear lives in the forests of South East Asia. It likes to make its home high up in the branches of trees. The sun bear sleeps or sunbathes by day and hunts at night. It has long, curved claws, which it uses to dig for insects. It also pokes its long tongue into holes in rotten wood to catch insects or lick up honey.

▶ *The sun bear's slithery tongue is up to 10 inches long.*

Foul fact!

If grabbed by the back of the neck, the sun bear can swivel its body around inside its loose neck skin to bite its attacker.

Ugly brutes

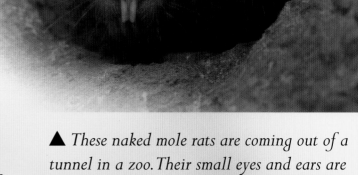

Some animals look ugly. They may have no hair, or have lumps on their faces, or be large and flabby with big noses. Although they look strange, these features are special adaptations that help the animals to survive.

▲ *These naked mole rats are coming out of a tunnel in a zoo. Their small eyes and ears are almost hidden in the folds of their skin.*

Naked mole rat

The naked mole rat lives in long tunnels in the grassy regions of eastern Africa. It lives in groups of 20 to 300 members, ruled over by a queen. Hairless skin means that the mole rat does not overheat in its underground home.

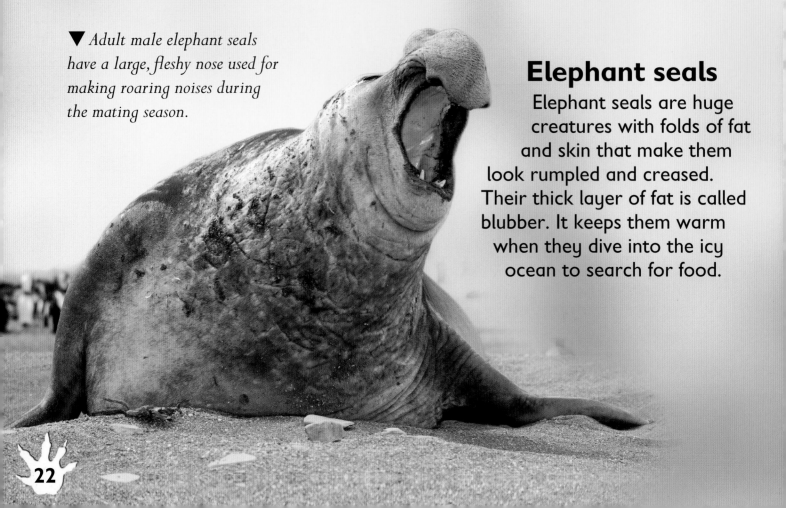

▼ *Adult male elephant seals have a large, fleshy nose used for making roaring noises during the mating season.*

Elephant seals

Elephant seals are huge creatures with folds of fat and skin that make them look rumpled and creased. Their thick layer of fat is called blubber. It keeps them warm when they dive into the icy ocean to search for food.

A warthog's canine teeth grow constantly. It uses them to dig and search for food.

▼ *The four hard bumps on the warthog's face cushion the blows when it fights.*

Warthog

The warthog belongs to the pig family. It lives in Africa. The male warthog has four hard bumps on its face that look like warts—from which it gets its name. Males and females have curved tusks, which they use as weapons, growing out of their mouths.

Gross eaters

Some animals have unpleasant eating habits. They may feast on dead animals, digest the bones of their prey in acid, or use their strong jaws to rip their prey apart.

▲ *The wolverine's sharp, powerful claws help it to kill prey such as rabbits.*

Wolverine

The wolverine is sometimes called a skunk bear or glutton. It lives in Alaska, Siberia, northern Canada, and Scandinavia. It often eats the remains of animals killed by wolves. It will also kill prey itself, by pouncing on an animal from a tree or rock, tearing it apart.

Pangolins

Pangolins are also called scaly anteaters. They live in tropical Asia and Africa, and are covered with brown scales. The pangolin eats termites, ants, and other insects, which it sniffs out and catches on its long, sticky tongue. It has no teeth. Instead, horny plates in its stomach grind down the food before it is digested.

▶ *The pangolin marks its territory by squirting a strong-smelling liquid from glands under its tail.*

Hyenas

Hyenas are strong, doglike creatures that live in Africa and India. Although they **scavenge** and eat carrion (dead animals), they also catch young hippos, gazelles, zebras, wildebeest, and antelopes. The stomach of a spotted hyena can hold up to 33 pounds of meat, so it can go for several days without food.

▶ *The spotted hyena uses its large jaws to crush the bones of its prey and tear through thick skin.*

Foul fact!

Hyenas have strong acid in their stomach. This helps them to digest chunks of meat and even bones.

Scary beasts

Frightening myths and superstitions have been created around some animals. But these stories are not true, and it is important to learn about these amazing animals.

Wolves

Wolves live in many northern countries. Gray wolves are fast runners, and chase down their prey. They hunt deer, elk, moose, hares, and beavers. In some places wolves kill farm animals and eat garbage from trash cans. Wolves live in packs of up to 20 animals. These packs are very close and organized: traveling, hunting, and raising families together.

◄ *Wolves have large, sharp teeth, which help to tear up meat.*

Aye-aye

The aye-aye lives in the rain forests of Madagascar. Using its long, bony middle finger, it taps on tree branches and listens for beetles and grubs moving under the bark. When it hears a grub moving, it picks it out of the bark using its long finger. It also uses its middle finger to scoop out the flesh from inside coconuts.

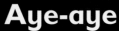

Foul fact!

Some people in Madagascar believe that a person will die if an aye-aye points its long middle finger at them.

▶ *The aye-aye's **habitat** is the tropical forest. It hunts at night in the trees.*

27

Make it!

Design an awful animal of your own. Will it have a nasty nose, a terrifying tongue, or special stink glands?

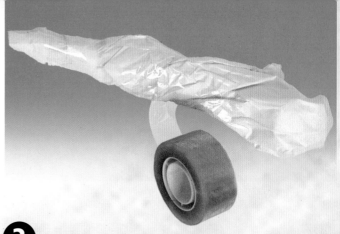

3 Screw up some paper to make the rough shape of your animal's head and body. Wrap sticky tape around the paper so that it holds its shape.

✂ *You will need:*

Paper
Pen
Sticky tape
Rolling pin
Modeling clay

Plastic knife
Large box
Paint
Leaves
Tissue paper
Card
Scissors

4 Use a rolling pin to roll out some modeling clay into a thin layer.

1 Make a list of all the features you would like your animal to have. Does it need slashing claws for digging in sand? How about a long, wobbly tongue for poking into holes to find insects?

2 Draw a sketch of your awful animal to use as a guide.

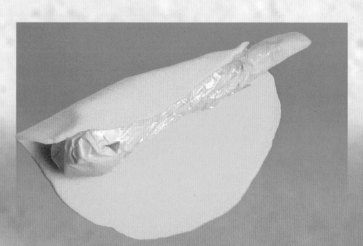

4 Wrap the modeling clay around the animal's paper head and body. Press the edges of the modeling clay together.

5 From another piece of modeling clay, cut out shapes for the eyes, tongue, and any other features, such as scales. Attach these to your model.

6 Make the creature's habitat from a box. Paint the box and decorate with leaves and tissue paper.

7 On a piece of card, write a display label explaining your animal's lifestyle and appearance, and attach it to the box.

Name: Statidraco
Size: 6.5 feet long
Weight: 154 pounds
Eats: juicy leaves and fruit, which it picks with its long tongue.
Habitat: grassland with scattered trees

Glossary

Appendage
A body part, such as an arm, leg, tail, or fin.

Bacteria
Very tiny organisms that can cause disease.

Biologists
Scientists who study the science of living things, such as plants and animals.

Bubonic plague
A serious, often fatal, disease caused by bacteria. The disease may be passed from rats to humans by fleas that have lived on infected rats.

Cub
The name given to the young of some animals, such as bears, lions, and tigers.

Den
Some wild animals make a den or lair in which to sleep, rest, or hibernate. They may use a natural hollow in the ground, or may build a den using leaves and branches.

Endangered
In danger of dying out or becoming extinct.

Extinction
When the last of a species dies, that species is said to be extinct. No more individuals exist.

Feces
Waste matter that passes out from an animal's anus.

Gland
A specific part of an animal's body that secretes substances.

Habitat
The natural surroundings of an animal.

Larva
The young of any invertebrate—an animal without a backbone, such as an insect. A larva is also the young of an animal that changes its form. A tadpole, for example, is the larva of a frog. Larvae hatch from eggs.

Mange
A skin disease in hairy animals, such as dogs, that is caused by a tiny parasitic mite. Animals with mange often lose their hair.

Mangrove swamp
A marine (sea-water) swamp found in tropical or subtropical places.

Northern hemisphere
The half of the Earth between the North Pole and the equator.

Parasites
Plants or animals that live by feeding on other living things. A tapeworm is a parasite that lives inside other animals and feeds on them.

Predator
A creature that hunts and kills other animals for food.

Prey
An animal that is hunted by another animal.

Roundworms
Any nematode (a type of worm with a rounded body) that lives in the intestines of humans and other mammals.

Rump

The backside or buttocks of a large animal.

Saliva

The liquid that forms in the mouth.

Scavenge

To hunt for and eat dead animals, or carrion. Vultures and hyenas are scavengers. They feed on the bodies of animals that have been killed by predators.

Sewers

Underground pipes and tunnels that carry away sewage from toilets and waste water from households.

Snout

The projecting nose and mouth of an animal.

Spur

A sharp, bony spike on the back of an animal's leg.

Suction

The act of sucking. Some animals have suction cups on their feet or legs that help them to grip their prey or slippery, steep surfaces.

Tapeworms

Long, parasitic flatworms that live in the intestines of animals, such as pigs, dogs, and humans.

Termite mound

Termites construct a nest about 3 feet below the ground. Above the nest, they pile up the earth into huge mounds full of tunnels, where they live.

Territory

An animal's territory is the area of land that the animal defends against other animals of the same species. Some animals mark the boundary of their territory with scent, and they hunt within that area.

Toxin

A poisonous substance, especially one formed in the body.

Typhus

A serious infectious disease caused by bacteria passed on by lice and fleas. It causes headaches, fever, and reddish spots all over the body, and can be fatal.

Venom

The poison used by some mammals, snakes, and spiders to paralyze or kill their prey.

Worming

When an animal is wormed, it is given a medicine that kills the parasitic worms living in its intestines.

Index